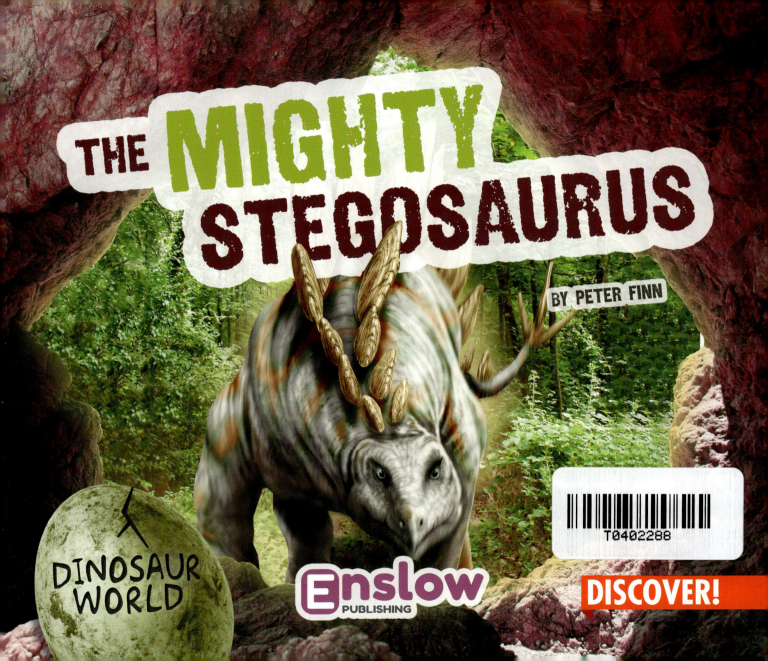
THE MIGHTY STEGOSAURUS

BY PETER FINN

DINOSAUR WORLD

Enslow PUBLISHING

DISCOVER!

Please visit our website, www.enslow.com. For a free color catalog of all our high-quality books, call toll free 1-800-398-2504 or fax 1-877-980-4454.

Library of Congress Cataloging-in-Publication Data

Names: Finn, Peter, 1978- author.
Title: The mighty stegosaurus / Peter Finn.
Description: New York : Enslow Publishing, [2022] | Series: Dinosaur world | Includes index.
Identifiers: LCCN 2020050630 (print) | LCCN 2020050631 (ebook) | ISBN 9781978521247 (library binding) | ISBN 9781978521223 (paperback) | ISBN 9781978521230 (set) | ISBN 9781978521254 (ebook)
Subjects: LCSH: Stegosaurus–Juvenile literature.
Classification: LCC QE862.O65 F555 2022 (print) | LCC QE862.O65 (ebook) | DDC 567.915/3–dc23
LC record available at https://lccn.loc.gov/2020050630
LC ebook record available at https://lccn.loc.gov/2020050631

Published in 2022 by
Enslow Publishing
101 West 23rd Street, Suite #240
New York, NY 10011

Copyright © 2022 Enslow Publishing

Designer: Sarah Liddell
Interior Layout: Rachel Rising
Editor: Therese Shea

Illustrations by Jeffrey Mangiat
Science Consultant: Philip J. Currie, Ph.D., Professor and Canada Research Chair of Dinosaur Palaeobiology at the University of Alberta, Canada

Photo credits: Cover, pp. 1, 5, 7, 9, 11, 13, 15, 17, 19, 21 (rock border) SirinR/Shutterstock.com; pp. 4, 6, 8, 10, 12, 14, 16, 18, 20, 22, 23, 24 (background) altanaka/Shutterstock.com; pp. 5, 7, 9, 11, 13, 15, 17, 19 (egg) fotoslaz/Shutterstock.com.

Portions of this work were originally authored by Brian Thomas and published as Stegosaurus. All new material this edition authored by Peter Finn.

All rights reserved. No part of this book may be reproduced in any form without permission in writing from the publisher, except by a reviewer.

Printed in the United States of America

Some of the images in this book illustrate individuals who are models. The depictions do not imply actual situations or events.

CPSIA compliance information: Batch #CSENS22. For further information contact Enslow Publishing, New York, New York, at 1-800-398-2504.

Find us on

CONTENTS

A Bony Back 4
Its Name 6
Plates and Spikes 8
Herbivore 10
How Big? 12
Not Too Quick 14
Babies 16
Where It Lived 18
Visit a Museum 20
Words to Know 22
For More Information 23
Index 24

Boldface words appear in Words to Know.

A BONY BACK

Stegosaurus was a large dinosaur. It lived more than 140 **million** years ago. It's famous for the bony plates on its back. The plates were shaped a bit like leaves. Scientists have a few guesses about what these plates were for.

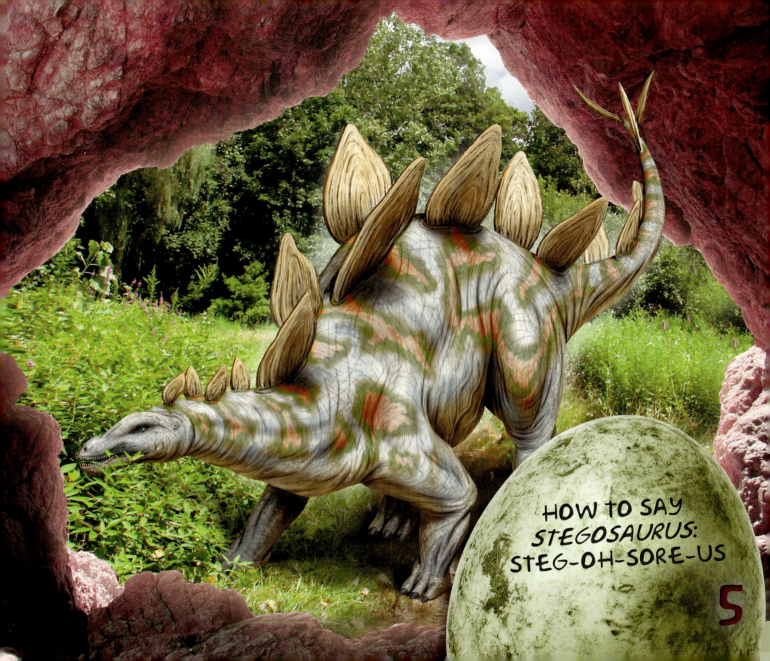

HOW TO SAY STEGOSAURUS: STEG-OH-SORE-US

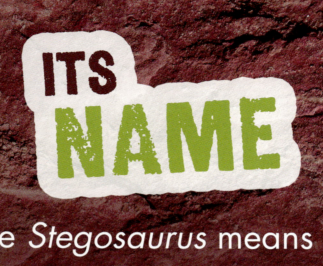

ITS NAME

The name *Stegosaurus* means "roofed lizard." At first, scientists thought the dinosaur's bony plates laid flat on its back. They thought the plates looked like tiles on a roof. However, they discovered the plates on its back stuck up.

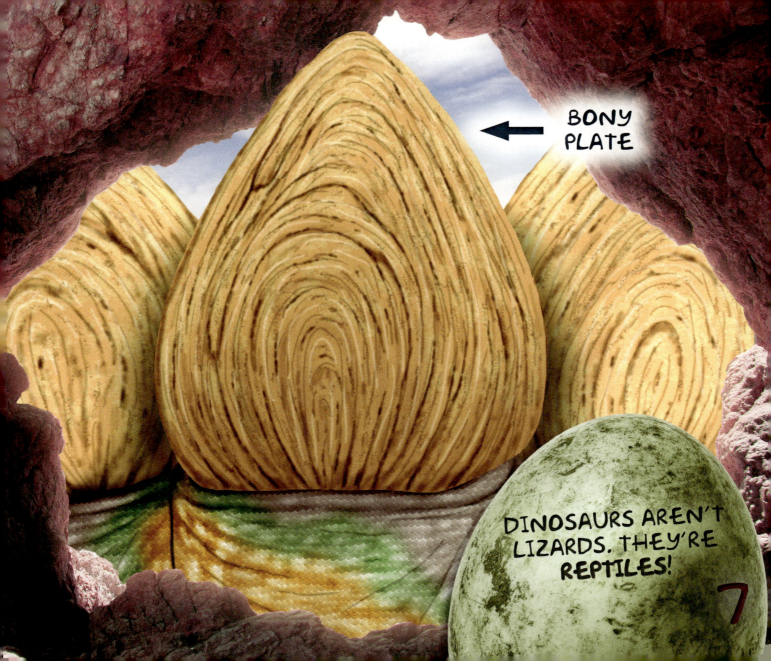

PLATES AND SPIKES

Scientists thought *Stegosaurus*'s bony plates **protected** it. Now, they don't think so. Plates might have helped the dinosaur keep its body the right **temperature**. Or plates might have drawn **mates**. However, *Stegosaurus*'s tail helped protect it. *Stegosaurus* had **spikes** on its tail!

HERBIVORE

Stegosaurus wasn't a meat eater. It was a herbivore (HER-bih-vohr). That means it ate only plants. It had a short neck. Its front legs were shorter than its back legs. *Stegosaurus* ate plants low to the ground, such as mosses and fruits.

SOME SCIENTISTS THINK *STEGOSAURUS* COULD STAND ON ITS BACK LEGS TO REACH HIGHER. OTHERS DON'T THINK SO.

How Big?

There were different species, or kinds, of *Stegosaurus*. The largest could grow to be 30 feet (9 m) long. They were about 12 feet (3.7 m) tall. *Stegosaurus* weighed more than 3,500 pounds (1,588 kg). That's as heavy as some rhinos.

NOT TOO QUICK

Not everything about *Stegosaurus* was big. It had a small, narrow head. That means its brain was small too. It wasn't very smart! *Stegosaurus* also wasn't fast. Some think it could only move about 5 miles (8 km) an hour.

BABIES

Scientists think *Stegosaurus* laid eggs in nests on the ground. The nests were made of dirt or plants. Then, baby *Stegosaurus* came out of the eggs. However, no *Stegosaurus* eggs have ever been found. Scientists have discovered baby *Stegosaurus* footprints, though!

WHERE IT LIVED

The first *Stegosaurus* **fossil** was found in Colorado in 1877. For years, *Stegosaurus* fossils were found only in western North America. In 2007, one was found in Europe. That means these two **continents** were connected at one time!

VISIT A MUSEUM

Stegosaurus fossils are in **museums** around the world. A nearly whole *Stegosaurus* fossil is in London, England. Scientists call it Sophie. However, they don't know if it was a boy or girl. There's much more to learn about *Stegosaurus*!

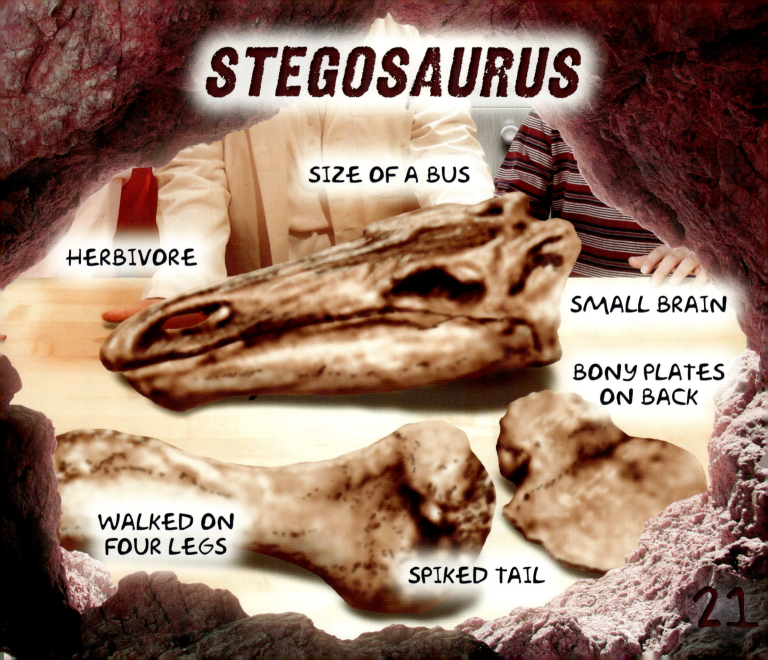

WORDS TO KNOW

continent One of Earth's seven great landmasses.
fossil The hardened marks or remains of plants and animals that formed over thousands or millions of years.
mate One of two animals that come together to produce babies.
million A thousand thousands, or 1,000,000.
museum A building in which things of interest are displayed.
protect To keep safe.
reptile An animal covered with scales or plates that breathes air, has a backbone, and lays eggs.
spike Something long and thin that ends in a point.
temperature How hot or cold something is.

FOR MORE INFORMATION

BOOKS

Carr, Aaron. *Stegosaurus*. New York, NY: AV2, 2021.

Radley, Gail. *Stegosaurus*. Mankato, MN: Bolt, 2021.

Ringstad, Arnold. *Stegosaurus*. North Mankato, MN: 12-Story Library, 2019.

WEBSITES

Stegosaurus
www.nhm.ac.uk/discover/dino-directory/stegosaurus.html
See how big this dinosaur was compared to a human.

***Stegosaurus* Facts for Kids**
www.sciencekids.co.nz/sciencefacts/dinosaurs/stegosaurus.html
Read some quick facts about this dinosaur.

Publisher's note to educators and parents: Our editors have carefully reviewed these websites to ensure that they are suitable for students. Many websites change frequently, however, and we cannot guarantee that a site's future contents will continue to meet our high standards of quality and educational value. Be advised that students should be closely supervised whenever they access the internet.

INDEX

babies, 16
back, 4, 6, 21
brain, 14, 15, 21
Colorado, 18
eggs, 16, 17
enemies, 9
Europe, 18
fossil, 18, 19, 20
head, 14
herbivore, 10, 21
legs, 10, 11, 21
London, England, 20

mates, 8
name, 6
neck, 10
nests, 16
North America, 18
plants, 10, 16
plates, 4, 6, 8, 21
reptiles, 7
size, 12, 21
species, 12
spikes, 8, 21
tail, 8, 9, 21